DRAWNDARK

DRAWNDARK

TONY ROBERTS

Shoestring Press

Printed by imprintdigital
Upton Pyne, Exeter
www.imprintdigital.net

Typeset by narrator
www.narrator.me.uk
info@narrator.me.uk
033 022 300 39

Published by Shoestring Press
19 Devonshire Avenue, Beeston, Nottingham, NG9 1BS
(0115) 925 1827
www.shoestringpress.co.uk

First published 2014
© Copyright: Tony Roberts

The moral right of the author has been asserted.

ISBN 978 1 910323 08 3

ACKNOWLEDGEMENTS

Acknowledgements are due to the editors of the following journals in whose pages some of these poems first appeared:

Acumen, Agenda, Critical Survey, Dream Catcher, Great River Review, The Interpreter's House, The London Magazine, New Walk Magazine, Poetry Review, Stand, The SHOp, The Warwick Review.

'Sea Monsters' appeared in *Poetry in the Blood* (Shoestring, 2014).

to Chris, Kate and Dan

CONTENTS

"The past is never dead. It's not even past." – William Faulkner,
Requiem for a Nun

DRAWNDARK

You are in and out of the room
undressing, night dressing, a toothbrush
in your mouth. The light is silvered.
You pause a moment – no toothbrush now –
and ask, 'Have you stopped reading, love?'
Yes I have stopped, puzzled at the word
'smokefall' – and then to watch you
as you move about the room.
I still adore this privacy
of seeing you in silhouette,
the dark repetition of these
nightly little ceremonies
calling forth new coinages: 'smokefall',
'drawndark', my heart a moonlit book.

THE POET'S FIRST WIFE

We, at least, are enjoying his performance,
his sensuality, his openness,
and I begin to wonder about her,
what she is doing, the poet's first wife.
She is weeding in the poem just now,
near the spot where he had earlier buried
the cat she loves, run over in her absence.

I turn to see his new wife looking on,
younger than him by twenty years or more.
Does it hurt her that he shares his first life
with an audience of strangers? Does she
marvel, as she listens with her fixed smile,
how a life can walk out on another life
and yet result in such iambic scars?

The poet's first wife is about to find
the reddish patch of earth which he has turned.
(He pauses for a sip of Chardonnay.)
Will she uncover it, her little corpse?
She will not of course hold him responsible,
though she might consider that it typifies
what is to her his patronising style.

Perhaps her stomach churns to see his name,
after all the heartache and whatever years –
the soil in the rumpled, bloody, brindled fur,
the twist of the neck, the yellowing bared teeth –
the poet's first wife who has lived with this,
this bullshit eloquence, his knowing sense
of audience; she who's heard it all before.

HOUSES AT NAPLES, 1782

for Charles Tomlinson

Through an oil sketch on paper
of crumbling masonry walls
pitted with scaffolding holes
we enter the silent kingdom
our notions of the past
worn as this washing slumped
in the windows of a still day.

AMERICAN BED

We lay these past few nights luxuriating in a huge American bed,
so wide we might as well be sleeping alone after all these years
and, as we cannot touch or turn against each other as we sleep,
our underwater dreams are largely undisturbed. This is a perfect bed
for falling out in, not for falling out of, though we fall neither in
                                                                nor out.

This bed is as wide as the Susquehanna, the Potomac and the
                                                    Rappahannock,
wide like the land we see as we see our children, their pasts in the
                                                            present.

Is everyone all right at home? Awake alone, I find my way to the
                                                        en-suite
by the bars of light through the blinds from the motel forecourt,
returning by the stars of refrigerator, clock and kitchen range.
I miss the ripple of your breathing as I try to settle this
                                            continent again,
then turn and turn in your direction, knowing you cannot be
                                                        far away.

MATTHEW ARNOLD IN NEW YORK, 1883

As we lay off Staten Island, the first light pale
   On an orné landscape of spires, villas, hills and woods,
      I jested, 'Not a single Mohican to be seen,'
   Which got into their newspapers. I know I should
      Have written sooner, Fan, but for the life marine.
         Our steamer swept out into such an Atlantic gale,
Odysseus himself might have been circumspect;
      Yet the crew proved masters of the situation,
      Showing 'self-reliance' beyond imagination –
Albeit we stayed bed-bound – waves thrashing the deck.

I have made time for the 'voice oracular's' essays
   And two volumes of his correspondence with Carlyle.
      The lecture is in my head, the passages marked,
   But how will I have time to write it, when all the while
      I live in a whirl – even since we disembarked –
         Writing nothing but my autograph each day?
I am advised to bar no-one, never left to myself.
      (The buoyancy and freedom from constraint here!)
      With such intrusive celebrity it should be made clear
That as Emerson noted 'The first wealth is health.'

As to the 'second' wealth: 'The Chicago Tribune'
   Claimed I have come for 'filthy lucre'. I concurred,
      But they may add to the charge now 'poor vocal pitch'
   For at Chickering Hall I was quite badly heard,
      Like the worst of the clergy, all mumble and twitch.
         I shall suffer the bile of their turgid lampoons
Until voice-training saves me – or the need is past...
      Yet they stayed to the end, according to Flu;
      So it is not quite (as yet) *tout est perdu...*
Here I sign myself Uncas – of the Mammon, the Last.

POEM TO A FRIEND FEELING OUT OF HIS ELEMENT

Turgenev tells of a little French drummer
caught by the peasants of Smolensk
after the sack of Moscow and how,
as they were preparing to cram him
down a hole in the Gniloterka River,
a passing farmer offered twenty kopeks
for the boy, believing by his wild mime
that he was master of all kinds of music.
The farmer warmed the drummer in wolf fur
and took him home as piano teacher
to his girls.
         There the boy was placed on
a stool before the shoddy instrument.
Impervious to the cheap perfumes
and the frou-frou of young ladies' skirts,
he finally and with deepest dread
plunged ahead, banging in his ignorance
on the keys as if they were a snare drum.
A sudden sinewy arm thrown round him
brought sensations of that coming ice,
but the farmer gave a grunt instead.
'I can see you know your stuff,' he said.

WAKING WITH HELEN

Last night you sewed your Helen costume
for the class assembly on the Trojan War.
(One little boy had to go home early,
after thinking too vividly on the event.)

Now in rosy-fingered dawn we lie drifting.
'Say something nice to wake me up,'
you murmur. 'Troilus has carved your portrait
in the most fragrant sandalwood,' I try

and then, receiving no audible response,
'The satyrs have forsworn all satiety
in honour of your day's festivities.'
'Is there something brewing?' you whisper.

Trouble? I think of bloody Agamemnon
and the Argive fleet knifing for Troy,
of Hector dragged through the dust in death,
of the Greek gift and Ilium's towers burning.

At that you open one azure eye and
searching my rumpled face for what is
playing there croon reassuringly,
'I was only hinting at a cup of tea.'

SEA MONSTERS

"Trelawny could not, even to save his life, tell the truth." – Byron

The *Bolivar* lay at anchor three miles off.
We were to swim to her, dine in the sea
alongside, treading water the whole while,
then return to shore, the weather calm.

I was by some distance the winner.
On the return Byron retched so violently
he had to be nursed back to the yacht
for brandy against the swim to shore.

He kept two days in his room, petulant,
with biscuits, soda-water and a drench
I administered, his lame lower limbs
soft and white as a crab's integrals.

No real swimmer, he, whereas Shelley,
who walked naked from the sea into
a dinner party, his brain absorbing him,
Shelley never flourished far from water.

STAGE WHISPERS

I want to show my daughter Life
   and so I take her to a play.
Being eight she makes a steamy choice:
   The Beggar's Opera by Gay.

And then in moonlight afterwards
   she lays her things beside the bed:
a fallen lock of Macheath's wig,
    a programme doomed to lie unread.

We talk of why they love Macheath,
   those ladies of the demi-monde.
She says, 'Because he brings them gifts.'
   And I, 'Because he's tall and blond.'

She takes my hand in both of hers,
   reprising Jenny Diver's role.
The knowing little minx is right:
   possession is what warms the soul.

TEMPS DE POISSON

Up in Maine one time and packing fish
four weeks under a guano-splashed tin roof
at a rusting, wet conveyor belt,
next in line to a student ballet dancer
with a turned-up nose; pulling swim bladders
out of headless whiting; packing them
crossways in waxed boxes for Vermont schools
('Our fish are dovetailed to perfection');
yelling 'gut bucket' when the box of pink
swim bladders fills; trying to beat the nimble
fingers of the oyster wives at the line head
before settling for state minimum;

smoking to Sparky's stories in the breaks;
reeling off the wharf with fish heads; gawking
at a two-hundred pound tuna on the deck;
chugging icy cokes and trying to get
the student ballet dancer in cut-offs,
with the bandaged thigh, to dump her handsome
giggling boyfriend; clocking in mid-mornings
and working on to chilly-fingered dawn,
cold and wet and hosing down the splattered wharf;
driving one-eyed to a rented mildewed
clapboard house, to beer and squid and sloppy joes
until roused from sleep and back to work again

and one time, when the guts wagon cab showed
three days late, the huge mound of gurry
turning truck grey, volunteering to shovel
it out at the dump – anything to get out
of the packing line for an hour or two;
having to slip and slide in rancid water
around the hill of guts; jabbing shovels

10

into its stinking bulk, releasing crazy
runs of maggots; coming home to burn the clothes
and stand for an hour in the shower
singing to the fish scales and pink bladder strings
John Denver's 'Country Roads', and in two weeks

only one free night for beer and pizza –
the one cop car parked outside the one bar –
with the student ballet dancer (of the nose
retroussé, cut-offs and the bandaged thigh)
a mermaid in her sea anemone
tie-dyed tee-shirt, dumping her giggling boyfriend
and slipping off with 'Pizza' Margarita,
leaving this limey tuna high and dry.

A GLASS IN DUBLIN

This is a sketch from Dublin, smudged in charcoal
on cartridge paper by an unsteady hand:
you are lying belly-up on one twin bed,
while the nearer boasts a huge M&S bag;
an umbrella flowers between. If buckets of rain
were pints of – What I am interested in –

you interrupt my doodling – are results
(the theme just now is 'losing weight').
I have returned from the Hugh Lane Gallery,
where the toilets are a work of art. Now I notice
how the wallpaper's vertical motif is reflected
in the mirror, like a smaller, thinner, tidier

Regency version of Sean Scully's stripes
and you in black jeans and white blouse
are – I see if I turn tightly in my chair –
also reduced to slimmer, chiaroscuro effect
in the mirror's stare. I point out
that it is all a matter of perspective, weight loss.

You peer at me disarmingly and sniff,
correctly assuming that this little piggy,
this blurred spouse, did not run all the way home,
but stopped at 'Fitzgerald's'. This is a cartoon of you
in Dublin as a reclining pint of Guinness,
late-modernist, expressionist, calorie controlled.

EPIGONE

Just then I cleared my throat and heard
    my father, dead at fifty-two,
      as if I'd flushed a rattling word
I'd loved and hadn't known I knew.

SELF-PORTRAIT WITH JACOB OCHTERVELT

Light finds its way directly, from a servant
seated in an upper chamber, down past
another, turning into shadow,
to illustrate a morning tavern scene.
A girl, egg-breasted, holds a feather
to the nose of a red-faced cavalier,
whose sottish friend has thrust a trumpet
to his sleeping ear. Is it Judgment Day?

A slight shift of position brings a second,
debauched subject into view: myself,
grizzle-bearded, reflected in the glass.
Either I have paid for all my nights
carousing till the second cock or it's
the work of unforgiving age, or both.
At any rate I enter my new decade
more and less myself, and wondering if

these scenes, these titillating allegories
of excess (whose well-lit outer chambers
hint at the drab order of our other lives)
preserve at least the glamour of idleness;
so that, despite ourselves, we warm to them,
to their stupors and stupidities,
in fact to the whole, unwholesome world
of cavalier gesture and Dutch courage.

SELF-PORTRAIT WITH PIETER DE HOOCH

for Pete Farrar

There's a wealth of imagination
in this Delft interior. It celebrates
the affluence of domestic space
with a suggestive scene involving
a cavalier, his hostess and her maid.

Check out the furnishings and fashions,
then follow the tessellated floor
inlaid with marble, black and white,
through a hallway to a high-back chair
in spring sunlight by a half-open door.

I think of this empty chair as mine,
with its partial view of courtyard
and that elm across the way. In fact
I've just stepped out into this thin day
to piss in the yard. Pete, wait for me. Ok?

HEALTHCARE

for the Grants and the Todds

No deer would venture into your garden
on the days of our visit. The squirrels
and chipmunk beneath your bird feeder
were inexhaustible, but no young deer.
We pretended we could see them, hiding
behind the hickories and sniggering.
Descending on Devils Backbone brewery
from the Blue Ridge this one afternoon,
discussing health and healthcare, we skirted
a black rat snake sunning in the road.
Taking another turn in that descent
we passed a bright red tractor-trailer
grinding up. Among things we should have done –
like meeting more often these past forty years –
was one you said as the semi revved by:
we should have sticked that snake off to the side.

CHARLOTTE BEREND IN NEW YORK, 1962

'Self Portrait with Charlotte Berend and a Glass of Champagne' by
Lovis Corinth, 1902

'And this Saskia,' Mama asked, 'was also nackt?'
'Not bawdy. Kein bisschen unzüchtig, Mutti.'
Sorry. We are all American these days.
I told her it was not disgraceful.
Of course this made no difference to Mama,
and so I must explain to her that, no,
Rembrandt's wife was not sitting naked
on his knee – though I was half-dressed, not nackt.
I was saying that the double portrait
had a long tradition. 'Only one name
glows in the darkness,' Lovis would say:
'Rembrandt.' We were honouring a master.
'A man who sold his wife's grave,' Papa began
and then stopped, because even he must concede
that Rembrandt van Rijn was a master.
'Yes, natürlich, while this is mere painting,'
he began again. 'True Art is of the past.
Mozart we listen to; Mahler we endure.'
Lovis would go with him only so far,
'We must have high esteem for the masters
of the past, or we should take a millstone
to where water is deepest.' Mutti would not
let go. 'But he is not nackt, only you are –
and look where his hand is.' Well, of course
his hand is on my breast in the portrait.
We were excited, 'newlyweds' as they say,
not moralising as Rembrandt would have been.
Now tradition itself is the dead weight.
(So much for Papa). Saskia died young.
Although he painted her much, she is never

herself, but always a figment of his theme,
of his imagination. I am at least
myself in Lovis' paintings, as in my own –
more than Mutti was, for all her fine clothes.

IN CHARDIN'S CARAFE

Stained in the umbers
of wall and table,
a reflection of a rim
of Seville orange
hangs like a goldfish

in murky water
beside uncertain images
of silver goblet
half-peeled lemon
and marbled pears.

Here in its exuberance
genius indulges
optical ambiguities
as stillness confounds
both eye and ear.

REQUIEM FOR A SISTER

Opus 80

Always this last image of her:
rinsing ivory-white fingers
in warm vinegar to invite
sensation. He cannot voice
despair except in this relentless,
accusatory tone. Mendelssohn,
his only consolation being
that when he's buried by his grief
this unambiguous music
will live to breathe 'ideas too de-
finite to be expressed in words'.

MARCEL AFTER MIDNIGHT

Having first composed themselves,
the members of the improbably named Quatuor Poulet,
their sheet music fluttering against furniture,
are performing the Franck 'Quartet in D major'
for that dying swan, Marcel Proust,
who lies across his brass bed
in the most attentive of postures.

We are on the Boulevard Haussmann,
in his cork-lined boudoir at one a.m.
There are plates of Legas powder (for fumigation),
memories of madeleine and lime-blossom tea,
bundles of *À la recherche du temps perdu*
alternatively stacked and strewn about the bed.

There are emanations, too, momentary motes:
Baron Charlus is listening amorously to Morel,
Swann to Odette, Marcel to the wayward Albertine;
Saint-Loup is whispering such lies to Gilberte,
while Madame Verdurin feigns boredom
with the Guermantes, who in turn are too preoccupied
to attend to Swann's reluctant explanation
that death will prevent him accompanying them south.

In his pictureless bedroom with the cream-coloured Empire wallpaper,
a black, tramless, treeless night barely visible
from its two blind windows,
Proust can neither hear his character creations
nor the commotion from the guns of Verdun.
Momentarily deaf to his imagination,
the poet inhabits only the music
('Proof of the irreducibly individual existence of the soul').

He will hear the Franck twice – for that larghetto!
And then, paying these handsome, put-upon young men
from a chinois casket plumped with fifty franc notes,
will bundle them off into four waiting black taxis,
these dishevelled musicians he recruited at midnight,
driven through the city, warm beneath his eiderdown,
a tureen of mashed potato – purée de pommes de terre – in his lap.

NIGHT AND DAY

I

You have been tapping your temples,
settling the extra-firming cream,
you explain, playing to my smile

and then you laugh. 'Oh God,' you say,
'I used day cream instead of night.
I might as well get up for work.'

Before you slip into our bed,
I watch my hand smooth down the duvet.
How habit-forming you've become.

II

'A giant's been here,' you call,
having surfaced from your dream
and slipped into the shower
to find the shower head
is almost out of reach.

Well I'm no giant, love,
and you're no water sprite

but I like the idea
of a morning open to
the possibility of a world
in which such wonderments
might wake and wash.

COLONIAL WILLIAMSBURG

We're dining on East India Company
Fried Chicken in the King's Arms Tavern
at lunchtime on Duke of Gloucester Street,
when a beefy actor in period dress
pulls up a chair and straddles the back.
'What think you, sir, of Patrick Henry?'
Our host counters with a question about
Henry's treatment of his poor, mad wife.

Aside from my embarrassed silence
('Give me Liberty or give me Death'?)
I'm left to wonder into what repair
the past has fallen. In this restoration
everything is colourful, upbeat
and well-maintained. Yet every artefact,
like all the talk, is of one time, that time,
a time which oddly seems to have no past.

SPIES AND COURTESANS

Sitting out an evening on the veranda
of the Baker house. Cicada, hot rain
and these alien, wet perfumes of summer.
Desire is a sixth sense by now. Army
sounds are muted: jangling harnesses, pickets.
We are reading behind each other's lines.
'Without decent maps the Union will founder
in Southern woods.' I rest on my cigar.
One lady present and the general
and two aides. The rhythm of her breathing,
the scent of her perfectly tapered arm.
Imagining its plumpness, the damp, light down
invisible to these ochre shadows.
The discomfort in the crotch, requiring
an unobtrusive re-orientation.

Returning the tea cup to its saucer,
to the grinding of ill-made crockery.
'There are two careers in Washington,'
the lady says, her lavender head inclined.
'All the gentlemen are politicians
or soldiers, the ladies spies or courtesans.'
A run of sweat between the shoulder blades
and tiny wing beats in my ear. An aide
removes a blanketing moth from the lamp.
His fingers halo red, then serve to light
the lady's kind, full face an instant.
'The talk at Willard's is "On to Richmond".'
'It is common knowledge that Willard's hotel
has more spies than bed linen.' 'And courtesans?'
General laughter. 'We must ask Mr. Russell.'

They turn their smiles to me. 'On the salary
of a correspondent, madam, even
a special correspondent for "The Times"
of London, I am sure that one has not
the wherewithal to pursue the question.'
'Why Mr. Russell, vous êtes célibataire?'
I turn the question with a hearty laugh.
Spirited, sturdy limbed and handsome
though, these American ladies. Courtesans
and spies? I am engaged, then, on two fronts:
this war and then a skirmish with the fair sex.
Ought I to linger, ask her if *she* pursues
a career, chance that old, well-travelled road
from correspondent to co-respondent –
oh God, did she just touch her hand to mine?

SPIRITS

Buried deep in cords of sawdust
in a schooner's lower depths,
ice bound for Secession ice houses
relives the lake where it was carved
in blocks the size of hay bales
and seasons flowing free and sweet
as apples cooling in the upper holds.

These autumnal, antebellum bushels
can anticipate the buttery light
of quiet, Charleston kitchens,
but summer's crop will find itself
in parlors foxed with candlelight,
on tables come alive with spirits,
with the great outpouring of the dead.

LOUIS & TRISH

I'm thinking of a plate stained by a crescent of yolk
from forty years ago and on it a fork with bent tines
as I warm my hands on a round brown teapot
after coming back to the flat from an afternoon session
at The Midland where Red John in his stained United tie
lets out a musical der der der der as the squad come in
and little twists of silver paper shoot everywhere
even across Len's wife who appears in the vault
slamming down his Sunday dinner shouting
'You bloody live here. Here's your dinner!' and him
not missing a beat 'Where's the salt and pepper love?'
while at that moment an escapee from the hospital
bursts in in his pyjamas, orders a pint which Stuart serves
since they've no dress code, and gets the head down
before two flushed nurses arrive Benny Hill style
and everyone boos as the redhead gives Stuart
a piece of her mind then shakes a fist at us
because the week before we've taken Patient Ken
to Band on the Wall – only he has no control
over his limbs – and though we have a great night
we leave him at the ward door because he's pissed
and 'One day' someone says as we're walking up
Palatine Road laughing 'wherever we are
we'll look back on this and laugh' and it's me
and I'm laughing still as I dry my hands at the sink
partly with delight at having them always here
and partly because – whatever anyone tells you –
I swear to God there's no such thing as the past.

A J&B FOR JOHN BERRYMAN

Ventured somewhat earlier this dark bar down,
his Pulitzer goin a dozen rouns with Cal.
'All is risk and variety'; thát you got right.
I hast it too now – Cawdor, Glamis & Crown –
& we'll *hiptohaunch* piss ... on Parnassus, pal.
Then blacks out he   malt & grainy the night.

THE DARK ONES

"How frightful and senseless, to link one's happiness with material
things – wife, children, health, riches." – Lyov Tolstoy

I told them we had lost a young mare in the lake
this winter past through utter, drunken carelessness
and that my mind will not release her frozen look.
They nodded but I saw they could not comprehend.

In their joylessness they lack vorstellungskraft,
these acolytes of his. I call them 'dark ones'.
The day brings two: one a spiny student from Kiev,
the other older, moon-faced. 'You needn't,' I said,

'look downhearted. He will soon return to tell you
how to live' – and then I wondered if the reason
for their coming was to get him to renounce
the copyright on his new work. I said instead,

'Today I took the children – those that you would rob –
to pick morels at Zaseka and now they're all out
playing pas de géant in the water-meadow.
It is a game I've spent my married life upon.'

I was clearly being too subtle for them. 'Do you read?'
I asked. I meant aside from His work. 'Spinoza
says that we must look for God not in miracles,
but in the everyday.' Again I drew blank looks.

I tried once more. 'He does not know the meaning
of "the everyday". Like you he lives toward some
future bliss.' Then I thought of Lyov's lechery
and what *La Physiologie de l'amour modern*

30

has not explained to me about sexual love.
I blurted out, 'If it is agony for him
to need his servants, what is it for me who have
to serve? Our warring visions of simplicity

exhaust us both.' I withdrew, expecting some response –
but no; they have no sense of the ridiculous.
And I? I've turned the key upon myself it seems,
to weep and watch her liquid eyes gel in my dreams.

ODYSSEUS ON RODOS

Once bitten, twice bitten
she stands at the foot of the bed
wrapped before the mirror
examining the damage done,
a study in soft, white towel
and wishful shades of brown

while he – two, three beers in –
lying pot-bellied naked
on their enchanting bed,
interrupts his posturing
to report a suspicious bug
now spiralling around her.

It disappears. He looks into
his 'Mythos': mystery solved;
the creature floats in its foam.
He flicks it out, reports it drowned,
rises above her ironic
celebration of his cunning.

A man skilled in all ways
of contending, he lies
contentedly appraising her
against the magnolia horizon,
the sweet prospect of a cotton
seagull's wing unfurling.

ORPHÉE ET EURYDICE (1859)

Ivan Turgenev to Pauline Viardot, preparing for her role as Orphée.

I miss Spasskoye's old, dark-gold alleys of lime
and the sudden cloudburst of nightingales,
water dripping from the muzzle of a cow
beside a pond, sunlight lagging on a lane,
birch buds, summer straw, wild strawberries.
My ache though is for you – at Courtavenel,
at Baden Baden, charades and cadenzas,
the scents and spirits of each vivid house.
We look back to place when we look to love –
recitative burnished to aria.
A day not opened by your eyes is lost.
If you will not take me,
   'Reçois donc mes derniers adieux,
   Et souviens-toi d' Eurydice.'

LOCUSTS

from the boyhood of Alexander Herzen

Perkhushkovo on the high road
standing in dusty fields, once maize,
our horses shat and shifted in a yard.
I took in stairs polished to bone,
forgotten footmen, old maids
who sewed and scolded pale boys.

They held me in this reliquary
and marvelled at how tall I'd grown.
We ate. My father passed out pleasantries.
They fussed. They scraped to kiss the hand
which he withdrew. Then we were gone.
'Estates,' he said, 'are eaten by their locusts.'

POSTCARD FROM BRUGGE

to Kate and Dan

To travel is to live both here
and there and now and then.
We watch flatlands flash past
from Brussels on to Bruges.

In the furrows of worked fields
lead white puddles; on the lips
of ditches pollard willows,
while dotted through wet pastures
the cows of Constable, de Cock.

See, we are so conditioned
by the galleries
that each northern landscape
is a homecoming.

HARRIET AND THE CROW

In black tracksuit bottoms
and blue tee-shirt, hair in braids,
  Harriet runs then skips,
watching her feet, to the neighbour's
  front path. There she locks her
little hands out in front of her
  and, advancing, alternates
her feet as if she walked a beam,
  before the quietest
of knocks. She takes a backward step
  and pivots slowly, finds
her balance, waits, returns and knocks
  a second time, turning
to reclaim her poise. The door opens
  and Harriet, arms swaying
behind her, fingers linked,
  asks for her big brother,
then dances off. A moment later
  he explodes across the lawn.

The street is thirty seconds clear
  before a crow drops down
like two squat fingers on a keyboard,
  grabs a pavement crust,
does its rolling walk and heaves
  up into an old rowan.

BURNS NIGHT

Louis' father sat reciting 'Auld Lang Syne'
and 'The Banks o' Doon' in my direction
as I stood in their front parlour, waiting
for his son to change out of his hangover.
He told me in that educated burr
how he'd recorded a selection
of the poetry of *Rabbie* Burns,
with incidental music played by friends
from the Hallé orchestra. Apparently
someone broke in and stole the finished tape.
I stood there, lost in thirst and sympathy,
until he added – as an afterthought –
that while the bugger had been up to it
he'd taken the new tape recorder, too.

LOVE,

Do you remember the old walled garden
of the pension at Cara dei Terreni
with the view over the Gulf of Salerno?
How formally it had all been laid out:
box hedges, pomegranate trees, hydrangeas.
And then the bats that came to bother us
and the olives we avoided then adored.
The twittering sisters and their charming,
dark-eyed brother: could they have been more friendly?

Of course you will not remember; after all
this was 1872 and the honeymoon
was not our own but Walter Crane's. Yet as I stood
in the shade of his watercolour, I thought
how we would have strolled, you and I, hand in hand
along the misty wall of that old mansion,
and how I would have taken you in my arms
beneath the orange disks of his pomegranates
and willed those awkward brushstrokes into life.

THE BUBBLE

"We are as bubbles which pop upon the surface of a raging ocean.'"
– Schopenhauer

I was busy conducting both sides
of our latest argument. *Besides,*

I smartly retorted just before
Blackfriar's Bridge. I hoped to score

by that sly adverb, since it seemed
to refer back to a point I'd dreamed

masking a solecism of mine,
when I saw the little girls in time,

their winter twin sets, on the town,
preoccupied, blonde haired, heads down

and then, as if sensing trouble,
I looked to see their work: a bubble.

What gives us pause? That silly slight
I'd emailed to you late last night,

some bubble in friendship, although brief,
bound to do a slight mischief

disparaging the great and good
with knocking quotes half-understood

on Derrida, Rorty and Arendt;
something I know I should not have sent

a lover of German thought and French,
of Heidegger ('philosophe, but mensch?').

Had I been with you, you'd be caught
half-standing, nursing the bruised thought –

with unlit cig – of my betrayal,
pausing on your way out to inhale.

You'd fix me like a cowardly dog
and then unleash your monologue

from that position, your half-crouch,
while I feigned calm upon your couch.

Well, life is short and then uncertain
(though it's not time to drop the curtain)

but still I'd hate a falling out
with so many other knots about.

I ducked to let the bubble coast
when all above me like a host

of seraphim more bubbles there
held soft formation in the air,

yet quivering like souls, all hope,
spherical films of air-filled soap,

eager and perfect in their way,
hovering towards Judgement Day,

speech bubbles, conceits by the score
soon scattered by the revolving door

expelling air from the Ramada Inn,
with stewardesses, one fat, one thin.

So George, I'm sorry for the trouble
of slipping in your thoughts a bubble.

An email will heal our spat no doubt
and my airhead thinking flow on out.

One day these girls will put by their toys,
their bubble guns and pursue the boys

and we will be what we will be:
bladderwrack bubbles on a raging sea.

GULLS

16/3/03

The cold has driven herring gulls inland.
   In the white morning sky
they circle our crisp little seas of lawn.

Half asleep, I think of trading places:
   territorial, suspicious,
we would sicken at their shifting point of view.

They would be worse off: clumsily caressing
   under heavy duvets,
clattering their wings against the banisters,

trying to make sense of kettle, toaster,
   and the morning headlines
wheeling and screaming as we flock to war.

MOMENT AT MAUBEUGE

It is 1914. Maurice Baring writes
of a 'tremendous moment' at Maubeuge,
seeing the arriving British troops
come swinging over a steep hill singing
'It's a Long, Long Way to Tipperary'

and how the villagers soon line the street
showering the troops with flowers and fruit.
They look so young, so 'invincibly cheerful'
that he slips into a shop to hide his tears
thinking of 'the undreamt of horror to come.'

I, worming into the space he's left behind,
am holding my wheezy breath in wonder,
little and spindly and madly waving,
until you are out of sight, Grandfather.

CICERO IN RECESSION

I scribble this to you even as I lie to lunch.
You will ask me where. Well then, with Volumnius
and two friends of yours, Atticus and Verrius.
Do you wonder at our lightness in such times as these?

The sultry Cytheris takes part as well. So, tell me:
does it amaze you, Cicero dining with an actress?
Of course they are habitually unemployed,
but what of the rest of us? Live in my books, you say.
You know I must be out of them, at least de temps en temps,
for conversation frees the tongue and so the spirits rise.

Just now I've told of how, when asked at last for questions
after interminable instruction, you replied
to the Philosopher that the question of dinner
had been praying on your mind. The question of dinner!

Books are everything – life itself – but even life
needs a little comestible flavouring at my age,
and so I read and write and dine wherever I am asked.
Besides, I've had to give up mourning the austerity
imposed upon this land by greed. Why expect justice
when all's connivance from our masters in the City?

Still, don't worry on account of my arrival.
A little frugality is in keeping with the times.
Prepare me sumptuous conversation then, in lieu.
They cook the books, perhaps, while we sit down to stew.

BASKETBALL

After registering at the Nueces Hotel
and before they went off to the recital
at which Rachmaninoff was determined
not to play that damned prelude again

'They lunched in the public dining room
on local avocados stuffed with lobster,
sea-food chowder and a health salad.
He smiled occasionally at his wife as he read
the menu to her, according to our reporter.
The meal over, he scribbled the $1.10 check,
leaving a 25-cent tip for the waitress'

Betty Persk, to whom the bellhop whispered,
'That sonofabitch had to be seven feet tall –
and did you get a look at those paws of his?
He must have played for the original Celtics.'

A VICTORIAN FLOCK

"I've thought of all by turns, and still I lie/ Sleepless" – Wordsworth

Look, here's Arnold sporting mutton chops
and Browning, roaring like a social lion.
There's Dickens, in the pink after his walk.
He stands with Allingham bending Ruskin's ear.
Tennyson will soon be drawing out his long,
Victorian afternoon at our expense,
with a reading that is sure to clear the room.

There goes Thackeray! Collins isn't far
behind with Mrs. Gaskell. Of course Leigh Hunt's
too busy cadging for his quarterly
and Rossetti has no eye for anything
except putting Miss Siddal at her ease.
Is that John Forster, deep in copyright?
And that, the other Hunt? I've seen Millais

exchanging *effi*cacious glances with
guess whose wife? Landor is here, not Italy,
George Eliot, too, back with Lewes from Weimar
and Julia Margaret Cameron
(Alfred claims her portraits give him bags
beneath the eyes). RLS has just arrived
with his short, American divorcée

a Mrs. Osbourne. He talks to Henry James,
his 'favourite adjective'. There's Sargent,
patiently enduring Whistler's envy
as Edmund Gosse expounds late Swinburne
to the 'inexpiable' man himself.
Mill is here, or hereabouts – I hear his voice;
he's holding forth among the blue stockings.

At length they tire of talking of themselves,
my eminent Victorians, and gather
at the patio, their attention fixed
on Nero, Carlyle's dog, who's busy
chasing his stubby tail around our Corolla...

How could I even begin to explain?
Better to turn over and try again.

THE *NOIR AMÉRICAIN*: WHERE HE SINGS
THE BLUES FOR LADY DAY

He's rehearsing with his new quartet, right?
But the drummer's all over everywhere.
So he's asking him where the fuck the beat lies
when Red comes in with the news that Billie's dead,
Billie Holiday. The beat stops right there.
He knew that she was back in hospital
and that she'd been arrested for possession
of narcotics in her goddamned bed.
But dead? He wonders what it is with God
that first he snatches Pres then gallops back
for Lady Day. 'Thrift, thrift, Horatio.'

He knew her on and off when she was living
at the Wilson. He had a chick lived there.
All three of them were into Chinese food.
They had a poky restaurant next door.
Billy lived on boiled rice and getting high;
she lived on Gordon's gin and Seven-up.
She also had a pimp who kept her poor.
On top of that the courts liked nothing more
than cutting up her cabaret cards.
And even when she could find work, the clubs
would claw some money back by hiring
local pick-up bands to play with her.

Europe might have saved her ass, like it did his.
In France they called him the *Noir Américain*.
He might be 'black', but he was treated white –
and they threw in the 'American' as well.
But they booked old Billie badly over there
and then the bastards turned around and axed
her tour. She had to work her passage home.

So what they had in common, then, was Pres,
that and a little flavoured rice. He even
spotted her a C note once when he was flush.
She kept her distance, though, given his rep.
One time she said this thing to him, she said,
'When I wear lacy pants, you'll be the first
to see 'em, Prince. Till then just keep that sweet tongue
and them endless fingers on that sax of yours.'

He'd seen her last his first week at the 'Five Spot'.
She looked a mess; she'd come on by to score.
His head, however, had been in... Elsinore?
Maybe he gave her cab fare, maybe. No,
not even that. It's a hole in his heart
this morning, having to remember that,
what with his fucked-up drummer reminiscing,
now Red has bought the news of her demise.

'Demise'. She'd like that word; she'd call it 'class'
because her life was mostly just being trashed
or tying tourniquets. She must have played
a thousand joints that wouldn't let her in
except as hired help. All those cheap hotels,
side doors and clubs she couldn't buy a drink in.
It's only natural she'd cling to any
little whiff of class that blew her way,
especially with that hard luck voice of hers.
Eat shit your whole life long, you're in for a whole long life.
Then weigh a little courtesy like 'Lady'
against all that and suddenly you're regal.
You become a thoroughbred of disdain –
a fragile one. He knows about that, too.
He's on a riff now, at the window there,
taking a time-out, looking down on garbage.
He lights a joint and holds the fire inside.

So if he gave her fuck-all that last time,
well then fuck him! We all father regrets.
All the sweet perfumes of Arabia...
The English call it 'letting the side down'.
He gives the phrase the air, with English spin.
Regret is hard to swallow, just like race –
except regret's a true democracy.
But Lady Day has gone and she could sing.
He takes the joint in little sips and smiles.
Shit, that's the truth, her singing, that's the truth.

IN WHICH HE JAMS WITH BIRD & HITS THE WATER RUNNING

So what's he playing at? He drank too much
and now he's sweating like a bastard. Why?
Because he's just about to share the stage
with Bird – with Bird, right? At the 'Open Door',
a bar/restaurant in the Village. A back room
jam session on a Sunday afternoon.
They tried him out an hour ago, gave him
some cockeyed riffs to play, some wild shit
the way they used to do at Minton's. He blew
them all away and now he gets to play
with that celestial, sure-footed cat
who can make even the loan sharks cry.

But this is some lugubrious venue, man,
a derelict ballroom, with a bandstand
and woodpeckered tables. Lotta anxious dudes.
He's just back from the head a second time
working his sorry way through smoke and sweat,
a haze of expensive booze and cheap perfume.
And then he gets the nod and it's his time.

Bird's blowing like a mother on 'Funky Blues',
the others falling all around him
as they try to milk the cat's inventiveness.
And one poor fuck is out to match him
note-for-note. Then suddenly the penny drops:
it's him. He is the flightless, fucking bird.
'Angels and ministers of grace defend us.'
Next thing a voice is chewing on his ear,
'Hey don't just do something, my man, stand there.'
The stage explodes in laughter and he's cooked.

He grovels on until the set is done,
then makes a bumbling bee-line for the door,
at which he gets the nod from Bird, who waddles
over shoeless – like Mister Five By Five
he's two men in his suit these days – and then
that husky voice which heralds sermon time:

'Hey don't you know that it's respect that kills?
Be bold; be resolute – and don't play me.
You got to show what's in that bag of yours.
Like your tone's your own voice, man. My fucked-up
history is in those licks. You don't want that.'

He rolls his sleeves and shows his needle tracks.
'See there's my penthouse, that my Cadillac.
These tracks you're looking at, they don't lead home.
I heard that you got something, man. No shit.
You're hungry, right? Well no-one gives a fuck.
Until young Lady Luck comes wiggling her ass,
you may just as well play with yourself.

Now how about you spot me ten? No bread?
You mothers have got nothing but your balls.
Stay cool. I gotta go and hock this horn.
Ain't mine'; he rounds his shoulder with those eyes.
'And man, just keep your mouthpiece safe, is all.
Finesse the rest – and off I deliquesce.'

The Prince 'debouches' into Washington Square –
among the pigeon shit and wino drool.
Did Bird really lay that sage advice
upon his head just now, or is he
improvising on the nod he got?
He squares his shoulders, finds his strut, takes off.
One thing he's learned from listening to the man:
you gotta keep your reed hard for the jam.

OF HOWLING AT THE MOON & DIGGING
BILL EVANS

So Thomas Hardy was a meliorist?
He sure the fuck is not. If anything he's
up for barking, baying, howling at the moon,
like that old schizo Pierrot in Debussy's
'Cello Sonata'. A meliorist?
Life is a crock of shit and that's the truth.
Take him, for instance. In this month alone
an old flame went out in the Atlantic

      Over the mirrors meant
      To glass the opulent
The sea-worm crawls – grotesque, slimed, dumb, indifferent.

Plus, they've suspended his cabaret card
and he's having trouble with Shirelle
and the cat is AWOL. Not only that,
his fifth floor walk-up's run by roaches.
Oh, and Rita Hayworth's married someone else.
So what the fuck's all this about Hardy?

Well, listen: at the 'Colony' last night,
a neighborhood joint in Bedford Stuyvesant
('Not a nice place, really', the English would say)
he's giving the ear to Miles' new sextet –
not out for crumbs or shit like that; in fact
he'd been doing all right at the 'Five Spot' –
until they grounded his sax. He doesn't need
a handout; he's just watching Philly work.

Anyway, he meets this white guy, sits down
practically on his knee, not seeing him
through clouds of Camel smoke. Obviously
the guy's nervous – hey, who wouldn't be?
They're giving him Red Garland's chair next set.

So the conversation's tight as Shirelle's ass.
Plus, anyway George Russell's with the dude.
(He's the deep cat who wrote a book he called
The Lydian Chromatic Concept of Tonal Organization.
He borrowed it one time to turn-on Marcie –
hell, the title would have been enough.)

It's only when this cat is up on stage
he clocks the name: Bill Evans. He has a way
of moulding to the piano and he plays
under the rhythm; there's poetry right there.
You can see that Miles is digging him.
They all are. This cat phrases just like Bird.

When the set is done they talk of this and that –
Debussy, Hardy – all those sheep and dales
and dairy maids and fate and shit. Like Brooklyn.
And then, when pressed, this cat articulates
the 'mission' that his music's taken on:
'to put emotion into the piano'.
What starts in technique ends in feeling.
Ok, the Prince digs that. The way he talks,
the way he looks, he'd pass for one of those
young science guys. He could have been in on
'Explorer 1' or one of Einstein's stunts.

In point of fact he's almost too cerebral,
except that this is what the Prince requires:
someone who can quote from Thomas Hardy
and will bust his chops as well. Like the Prince.

This is a guy, George says, with bookcases!
A guy who reads Kafka, Sartre, Freud and Zen.
This is the kind of guy who plays piano
with Debussy sitting in his pocket.
He can see it now: *classical* jazz,
played by Ty 'Prince' Dove and plain Bill Evans.
(He'll bring the blues). He can almost hear

the purists moan, those dicks who like to think
that white musicians are a brand dilution.
That's jazz as coffee. You can serve with cream
but its natural flavor's black. Fuck 'em!
Like Miles, *his* thinking's light years ahead.
This white cat's offering something new.
One thing though: he needs to lighten up.
He listens too intently – they'll rib him raw.
See how tonight the Prince has stopped *his* howling;
that's self-restraint. 'The readiness is all.'
What this cat needs is the Prince to be his guide.
(He'll need to spirit him away from Miles.)
They'll meet where Africa and Europe meet.
Shit, it'll be the Convergence of the Twain.